It is the ferment of Love that fell into

the wine

                                                   Rumi

Only Garden of Roses

Copyright © 2015 by Alireza Ahmadian Zarchi
All rights reserved. This book or any portion thereof may not be reproduced or used in any manner whatsoever without the express written permission of the publisher except for the use of brief quotations in a book review.
Printed in the United States of America

First Printing, 2015

ISBN 978-1-329-10324-5

Email: Alireza@ahmadian.com

Conflicts of Family Law in Islam and Iran

(Hermeneutical Review of Financial Relationships of the Wife and Husband in Islam and Iran Family Law)

By:

Alireza Ahmadian Zarchi

Dedication and Acknowledgement

I would like to dedicate this book to **Haj Sheikh Jafar Mohajeri**. He has shown me the path to enlightenment and has aided me greatly in my endeavors to become a better person.

Contents

Abstract

Dedication and Acknowledgement

Student's Declaration

Contents

Introduction

   Limitations

   Methodology

Chapter One

The Marriage Portion (*Mahriyah* or *Mahr*)

   Introduction

   Religious Decrees and Family Laws

   1. *Mahr* and its Types

   2. Permanent and Temporary Marriages without *Mahr*

   3. Amount of *Mahr* without Initial Determination (*Tafwid Bud'*)

   4. Payments Other than *Mahriyah*

   5. Specification of the *Mahr* by a Woman by Power of Attorney

   6. Payment of Half the *Mahr* to the Husband

   Results

Chapter Two

The Daily Expenses (*Nafaqah*)
  Introduction
  Assessing the Rules
  1. Conditions for Paying *Nafaqah*
  2. *Nafaqah* for Permanent Marriages
  3. Obedience and *Nafaqah*
  4. Amount of *Nafaqah*
  5. Daily *Nafaqah*
Chapter Three
Wages for Housework and Work outside the Home
  Introduction
  Assessing the Rule
  Results
Conclusion
Bibliography

Abstract

Islam holds the family in high regard. Because many individual and social relationships derive from and affect the institution of family, Islam bestows the highest importance to this social unit. Consequently, the basic reality of family, spousal relationships, and safeguarding of intimacy and friendship within the family are subjects of great significance. A major component of family matters is the financial relationship between husband and wife. Appropriate attention to this aspect of the family may smooth the way to preserving family cohesion in a worthwhile way.

Marriage portion, financial support, housework, and work outside the home are among the major economic affairs in marriage. These are so important that through correct management thereof, a family may satisfactorily sustain its existence. They may even compensate for problems in other areas of married life such as shortcomings in marriage etiquette and sexual relations. These financial problems among spouses have been studied and assessed in three separate chapters entitled 'The Marriage Portion (*mahr*)', 'Daily Expenses (*nafaqah*)' and 'Wages for Housework and Work Outside the Home'. Along with introducing existing problems in each chapter, relevant Islamic decrees and family law codes have been analyzed. The Islamic decrees, with over 1400 years of history, have been chosen as the standard of this comparison and dissimilarities with the relevant legal codes have been discussed.

The marriage portion (*mahr*), specified at 500 dirham (about $1000) by Islamic decree, is assessed in the first chapter. It is highly recommended not to exceed this amount. When the wife specifies the amount of the marriage portion on behalf of both husband and wife in the case that the marriage formula has already been read, she cannot specify over $1000 and, even if she does, the marriage portion is still only $1000. This shows the importance of specifying the least possible amount for the marriage portion; however, this has not been mentioned in Iran's family law at all nor has any limitation for the marriage portion been explained therein.

In the second chapter the duty of a husband to pay daily expenses (*nafaqah*) has been discussed along with an analysis of reasons husbands have difficulty paying it. Obedience to the husband by the wife is the leading grounds in Islamic decrees for entitlement of the wife to receive *nafaqah* although such sensitivity cannot be witnessed in Iran's family law.

Performance of housework in the husband's home entitles wives to a suitable wage. This issue has been analyzed in the third chapter. The Iranian culture does not have the convention (*urf*) of paying wages for housework; however, this is considered very important in Islamic decrees. Unfortunately, this issue has also been neglected by lawmakers and is only dealt with when the wife is divorced by the husband.

In each chapter supporting and opposing opinions of scholars have been analyzed and some solutions offered, including limitation of the marriage portion and enacting laws that clarify obedience of the wife and that provide incentives for paying monthly wages to wives through banking systems.

Introduction

The institution of the family has a key role in the success or failure of a society (Mohammadi, 2004) and a proper financial relationship between a husband and wife is one of the major fundamentals of the success of this institution (Anon., 2013).

Islamic decrees, which have been practiced for over fourteen hundred years, have entered a new phase in recent decades with the rise of modernity. The law of Iran, which is based on religious decrees, started introducing new legal codes from outside of the religious framework and from that time imbalance and confusion have been introduced into the law. The family institution had to tolerate harm from both the present-day destructive morality and the confusing law as well. The law, which was supposed to encourage marriage and the family institution, has turned into a tool of separation and divorce (Parsa, 2001). Major problems between spouses that are related to the current family law exist in the area of finance mainly with regard to the marriage portion (*mahr*), daily expenses (*nafaqah*) and wages for housework. Each of these three items alone is enough to discourage young adults from getting married or bring about a collapse in the marriage and/or divorce among already married couples.

The marriage portion, which is a beautiful tradition set by the Prophet of Islam for giving a gift of kindness to one's wife-to-be, has turned into a tool used by some wives to exact revenge at the needed time (Damad, 1990). The marriage portion, in an amount up to $1000, is supposed to sweeten the life of newlyweds; however, since it has increased up to tens and even hundreds of thousands of dollars, it has only gifted bitterness from the very outset of married life.

Nafaqah, which is money for daily expenditures, is supposed to be given cheerfully by husbands, but in recent times its payment has been subjected to doubt because of the disobedience of wives. Men doubt their obligation to pay the expenses of the marriage, which is supposed to be a joint partnership with complimentary rights, and prefer to terminate married life which is nowadays a life full of contention and disobedience only expecting money from them (Kariminiya, 1998) . *Nafaqah* is to be paid in a situation where the wives can present a happy life to their husbands, children and the society by obeying their husbands in the marital relationship and choosing a happy approach towards their husbands.

Iran's family law, which has taken a strict approach towards the husbands' duty to pay the daily expenses (*nafaqah*), has set aside and forgotten the duties of wives concerning obedience to their husbands. This oversight of the law has resulted in women assuming *nafaqah* to be the absolute duty of husbands while considering their own obedience to be only a recommended ethical behavior and not a condition of the religion and the law for payment of daily expenditures (Allaee, 2004).

Another issue concerning financial problems is wages for housework done by the wife. According to both Islamic decree (Khomeini, 2002) and family law

(Mansour, 2012), a wife has no duty to perform the housework and, if she does, she is entitled to be paid a wage. The matter of paying a wage to one's wife is very strange and new to the conventions (*urf*) of Iranian culture and some scholars even claim that if women marry under the current culture and conventions, it means that they have accepted the condition of doing housework as a part of their duties without any wage (Taheri, 2009).

Some double-standards between Islamic decrees and family law have caused chaos among Muslims—who are wondering whether to follow Islamic decrees or the country's legal codes—along with instability in marital life. The absence of firm harmony between Islamic decrees and legal codes has resulted in imprisonment of many husbands by their wives who either abuse the law or really think they have the right to force financial support without any reciprocal duties.

If the lawmakers can secure the financial affairs of wives properly, family dysfunction caused by conflict regarding financial issues will dissolve and disappear. By amending the family codes it can be hoped that women achieve their financial rights and men face less pressure in this regard.

The Islamic decrees with regard to the marriage portion, household expenses (*nafaqah*) and wages for housework have been compared with related codes of Iran's family law in three separate chapters and various opinions of the scholars have been analyzed and studied. A hermeneutical approach based on the classic method has been practically followed together with reconsideration of Islamic decrees and legal codes.

The main goal of the producer of a text will be studied using classic hermeneutics and the impact of the time and place will also come under consideration (Shabestari, 2010). It has been attempted to discover justice as the main goal of God (Mutahari, 1980) by reassessing and reinterpretation of Islamic decrees and legal codes.

The significance of the present research is that through investigation and analysis of the relevant Islamic verdicts regarding financial concerns of spouses in the present age, many marriage complications may be rectified, thereby substantially decreasing the number of divorces and helping marriages among young women and men to thrive.

In this dissertation, I will investigate some of the important financial verdicts of Islam that pertain to husbands and wives, including the marriage portion, financial support for daily expenditures, wages for housework, and work outside the home. Existing problems in the views of both women and men will be discussed and potential solutions will be put forward.

Limitations

Due to connection of this research with the family law of a particular geographical area, i.e. Iran, this research was limited the research, articles and thesis that could be utilized.

This also means the present research mainly utilized resources which were in Persian, but also made use of several works in Arabic which were involved with the religious decrees discussed herein. The official religion of Iran is Shiite Islam, and the related family law is based on this school of thought. Therefore, this dissertation was delimited to examination of Shiite decrees on the topic at hand. Analyses and assessments in this research was based on other theoretical opinions and research. Due to the lengthy procedure for getting permission in practical surveys in family courts, this research could not take advantage of opinions of divorced couples concerning the theoretical analyses brought forth.

Another limitation concerns the actual value of five-hundred dirhams (one kilogram of silver) which was set by Prophet Mohammad as the marriage portion for all his wives and became a tradition for Muslims. The power of purchase of fourteen hundreds years ago in comparison with today needed to be determined based on one kilogram of silver so the analysis of the marriage portion could have a definite outcome. This limitations means that the marriage portion stated in this research cannot be considered definitive.

Methodology

The employed methodology is based on the goal of the research, which is reducing the divorce rate and increasing the marriage rate.

The present problem in Iran's society is that the rate of divorce has increased and the marriage rate is falling. According to statistics, the majority of divorces are based on financial issues. Many of these problems are due a combination of Islamic decrees with secular legal implementations, leading to imbalance in Iranian family law.

Relevant financial decrees have been assessed and compared with related family law codes. The philosophy behind this comparison and assessment is to discover differences and their severity. It is obvious from divorce statistics that the majority of divorces are connected to areas of the family law that have deviated from the aims of religious decrees.

The opinions of the clergies (*maraji*) and scholars of law have been analyzed. Supporting and opposing opinions have been assessed along with the opinions of the author of this research. Possible solutions have been presented.

Chapter One

The Marriage Portion (*Mahriyah* or *Mahr*)

Introduction

Mahriyah is an Arabic word meaning *to show love and to gift* (Zubaidi, 1987). Other synonymous Arabic words include *ṣidāq*, *naḥlah*,[1] *farīḍah*, and *ajr* (Tabatabaii, 2000). However, in Islamic parlance, *mahriyah* is an amount of money or property that a man bestows upon his wife at the time of the marriage ceremony (Khomeini, 2004). It is similar to *thaman* (a price) in transactions, though it is also different in some ways.[2]

---

[1] This word is derived from the root *naḥl* meaning bee. It means to gift since the work of honey bees is based upon gifting (Raqib, 1983).

[2] However, some scholars including Mullā Muḥsin consider *mahriyah* to be fundamentally different from *thaman* in other contracts (Feyz, 1983). Regardless, the main difference between *thaman* and *mahriyah* is that if *thaman* is not honored in a contract, the contract becomes invalid; however, if *mahriyah* is not honored, the marriage agreement is not invalidated (Khomeini, 2004, p. 92).

The marriage portion (*mahriyah*) is one of the basic pillars of marriage such that every marriage consists of *mahriyah* even if an amount has not been specified for it or if it has been rejected as a component of marriage. Though it is a basic element of marriage, it has been formulated such that it does not compromise the marriage itself. Therefore, negation of *mahriyah* or indeterminacy thereof, does not undermine the marriage contract (Makarem, 1996).

Islam's original purpose for *mahriyah* in marriage, which is nowadays usually determined in the form of gold, was to create love between the spouses (Imami Namini, 2006). In all cultures of the world, a form of gift giving by the husband, wife, or both is customary at the start of marriage (Azizi, 2003). As a virtuous tradition, Islam not only recommends but requires that a husband give a small gift—small meaning a gift that will not cause him economic or mental pressure—to his wife at the start of marriage. Of course, a woman can absolve her husband of his obligation if she so desires (Al-Amili, 1983).

In his time, the holy Prophet (s) advised an equivalent of 500 dirhams[3] for *mahriyah* and determined this same amount for all his wives (Ameli, 1967). Five-hundred dirhams is approximately worth 1,250 US dollars in modern times. The amount has been established such that it is neither derisive or offensive to a woman nor so high that a man cannot afford it. Thus, it is a gift that considers both aspects. Historically, some religious authorities have necessitated this exact amount, considering any greater amount to be haram (Seyyed Murteza, 1996). Most, however, have considered sufficient a strong recommendation against (*makruh*) greater amounts. Recommendations for low *mahriyah* can be found in many hadith by the Prophet (Ò) and Imams ('a). In one such hadith, it has been stated that the worst women of the ummah are those with high

---

[3] Every dirham is equivalent to 2.5 grams of pure silver. Thus, five-hundred dirhams would be equal to 1.25 kg of pure silver which is worth close to 1,250 dollars (silverpriceoz.com, 2013).

mahriyah (Ameli, 1967, p. 163). Furthermore, Imam Ali ('a) has stated that excessive *mahriyah* results in arguments or quarrels (Ameli, 1967, p. 191).

In modern times, the amount of *mahr* has increased greatly such that 300,000 dollars is a common figure and sums of 50,000,000 dollars have been seen (Yousofzadeh, 2005). Obviously, this inflated amount cannot be seen as a gift since the majority of men cannot bestow such large sums at the time of marriage. In this case, the *mahr* becomes a debt to the wife, causing future disputes.

The following may be some reasons for the high sums determined for *mahriyah* in recent times (Zarchi, 2012):

1. Weak faith in Islamic precepts
2. No economic support for women during and after marriage on the part of her parents and the society
3. Lack of marriage security and peace of mind due to high divorce rates

4. Islamic license for men to have more than one permanent wife
5. Islamic license for men to enter into temporary marriages
6. Ease of divorce for men
7. Lack of ethical conduct among men such as the tendency towards addiction to narcotic drugs, alcohol, and other things

The above items may be considered as the major reasons behind the endeavors of women to increase their *mahr*. They use this method to increase their peace of mind and achieve economic security so that, in the case that their marriage ends in divorce, the woman does not fall upon hard times.

Though the items above are true, the increase in *mahr* has not been successful in the role as a preventive since such a role was not assigned to it. Attempting to use *mahriyah* in this role is similar to trying to play soccer with a table tennis ball.

The preceding issues have resulted in much harm to women. However, all these matters cannot be compensated and such occurrences cannot be prevented using *mahr*. In addition, a result of the inflation in the amount of *mahr* is that *mahr* itself becomes one of the most significant causes for divorce increasing harm to both spouses (Iranian Drug Control Headquarters, 2013).

Family law in Iran, which is more or less representative of related Islamic precepts, has not been able to confront the current reality of ever-increasing divorce and adapt itself to it (Avvo, 2012).

The significant sums of *mahriyah*, which initially had no effect on men's decision to marry, have now become so paramount that every man must seriously think about this matter before deciding to marry. Hence, the new generation of men question and sometimes even all out reject the very concept of *mahr*. Iranian Muslim men question the reason behind these monetary requirements in married life, which is supposed to be based on mutual collaboration and sharing.

The ultimate purpose of this dissertation is to hermeneutically study Islamic law and Iranian law in regard to marriage. In line with this, the purpose of this chapter is to determine an amount for *mahr* and eliminate or mitigate challenges on the path to marriage.

Much the same as other economic issues examined in this book, *mahr* has become a deterrent in achieving sustainable marriages. In tandem with other economic issues as a collection of economic problems, it impedes marriage and facilitates divorce.

By examining Islamic decrees and Iranian family law regarding the marriage portion side by side, perhaps the causes of these problems may be found. It may be that though many rules have been formulated in Iranian law, the basis and purpose of *mahr* according to the religion have been completely disregarded.

Religious Decrees and Family Laws

In accordance with Islamic decrees, *mahriyah* is an important economic tradition in marriage. The Quran (2:237,[4] 4:4,[5] and 4:24[6]) and many hadith have highlighted this issue.

In this chapter, as well as all other chapters of this dissertation, the jurisprudential framework is based on *Tahrir al-Wasilah* by Ayatollah Khomeini.[7] Relevant decrees are compared with articles of Iran's family law.[8]

---

[4] "And if you divorce them before you touch them, and you have already settled a [dower] for them, then [pay them] half of what you have settled, unless they forgo it, or someone in whose hand is the marriage tie forgoes it. And to forgo is nearer to Godwariness; so do not forget graciousness among yourselves. Indeed Allah watches what you do" (Qarai, n.d.).

[5] "Give women their [dowers], handing it over to them; but if they remit anything of it of their own accord, then consume it as [something] lawful and wholesome" (Qarai, n.d.).

[6] "...As to others than these, it is lawful for you to seek [temporary union with them] with your wealth, in wedlock, not in license. For the enjoyment you have had from them thereby, give them their *Mahr*, by way of settlement, and there is no sin upon you in what you may agree upon after the settlement..." (Qarai, n.d.).

[7] The Islamic decrees will be taken from Tahrir al-Wasilah by Ayatollah Khomeini whose book is generally used as the main reference for Islamic decrees, especially in the lack of relevant laws according to article 167 of Iran's constitutional law.

1. *Mahr* and its Types

Anything a Muslim can own may be specified as *mahr*....Moreover, it is recommended (*mustahab*) that its value be no more than the amount determined by tradition, i.e. five-hundred dirhams (Khomeini, 2004, p. 92).

Mahr must be determined in a way that is not vague....However, it is not necessary to specify it as in transactions and other exchanges (ibid).

Article 1078: Anything possessory that can be owned may be specified as *mahr* (Mansour, 2005).

Article 1079: *Mahr* must be made clear enough that the two parties know what has been determined (ibid).

---

[8] Because *mahr* is an extensive jurisprudential subject, only religious decrees apposite to the purposes of the current research are discussed herein.

> Article 1080: In determination of the amount of *mahr*, both parties must reach an agreement (ibid).

It is not *mahr* itself that has caused the previously mentioned problems in Iran but its considerable amount. Thus, prompting the question by men, "Why should men have such weighty responsibilities so one-sidedly?" (Mahdavi, 2007). In the third millennium, a time when the equality of men and women is unceasingly being considered and researched, how is it that men must accept these difficult burdens?

Unfortunately, family law in Iran has implemented Islamic decrees regarding marriage in an unprocessed and fragmentary manner. Many shortcomings exist in the area of *mahr*, causing extensive problems. In the religious decree above, the five-hundred dirham recommendation was presented initially and is indicated many times in subsequent decrees. In some cases, it is considered the only criterion for figuring the marriage portion. However, family law lacks any consideration of this and the amount of *mahr* has not been limited to this extent.[9] Of course, Imam Khomeini has presented the five-hundred dirham limitation as a recommendation. However, others such as Seyyed Murteza (1996) have considered it haram to deviate from this figure. Katouziyan (1998) and Damad (1990) believe that there should be no limitation for *mahr* and that family law is correct on this. They maintain that determination of a limit for *mahr* would be excessive interference by legislators in personal issues (ibid). Ghafariyan (2011) and Habibi (2003) oppose this idea, stating that lack of interference by the government leads to higher divorce rates and increase in the number of men incarcerated due to inability to pay *mahr*.

Even so, Ghafariyan (2011) and Habibi (2003) do not emphasize the enactment of a five-hundred dirham limit on mahr. They propose limitation of the marriage

---

[9] In 2011, a law was passed that only marriage portions up to 110 minted gold coins are open to litigation (Bahonar, 2011). This law was essentially a positive movement. However, it turned out poorly since it sought the aims of the religion inadequately. One-hundred and ten gold coins is still a high sum for youths seeking marriage.

portion on the basis of the traditions of each city, city classifications, and other factors. The end result of their methodology is a chart determining the figure of *mahr* with regard to various factors such as level of education. In effect, this classification of cities and levels of *mahr* precipitates a class-based view of the society, impacting social justice. Habibi (2003) does, however, believe that the 110 gold coin limit in the new law is appropriate. Recently, a law was passed requiring a *mahr* of 110 gold coins for legal action (Bahonar, 2011). Previously, all marriage portions were actionable and the husband could be incarcerated if he could not make payment.

The second religious decree noted above presents an interesting point. It is not necessary to clarify the exact amount of *mahr* as in other contracts; seeing the *mahr* is sufficient. This means that even if a woman does not know the exact amount, e.g. weight and dimensions, and has only a general perception of the *mahr*, it is sufficient. This and subsequent decrees make it clear that *mahr* is not a prime concern of God, the Legislator. He has determined it as a gift rather than a price (*thaman*) in a transaction (Damad, 1990, p. 231)

Marriage possesses such importance in Islam that the Legislator has endeavored to present *mahr* as a simple thing so that it does not impede this advantageous bond. With this perspective of the religion, which alas has been neglected in the text of the law, the question asked by the generation of the third millennium is automatically answered. Giving a gift of around one-thousand dollars would not be a major cause for men to protest and courts would no longer rule to incarcerate a man who cannot give the determined amount of *mahr*. Marriage rates will increase and divorce rates will decline due to the absence of *mahr* as leverage.

Islamic decrees denote that a general understanding of the amount of *mahr* is sufficient and also that education or instruction can be determined as *mahr*. This plainly shows that *mahr* is not a matter that should necessitate court battles or hinder marriage.

Most importantly, according to the religious decree above and article 1078, *mahr* must be possessory and executable. Therefore, a *mahr* that cannot be given is void and must be replaced with *mahr al-mithl* (fair dower). The *mahr al-mithl* is determined according to custom and common practice. For example, specification of *mahr* as the Caspian Sea, an arm and a leg, or a mountain of gold is invalid since they cannot be delivered. Such a *mahr* is substituted with a *mahr al-mithl*.

Consequently, it can be assumed that many of the marriage portions recorded in marriage notaries are legally void since the majority of youths are not solvent enough to give on demand a *mahr* of several hundred thousand dollars to their wives. In addition, *mahr* is usually specified in gold coins which increase in price along with inflation. Therefore, even if a man works his entire life, with the high inflation in Iran, he will not be able to present his wife her full *mahr*. This distinctly shows that current marriage portions cannot be handed over and are thus null and void.

2. Permanent and Temporary Marriages without *Mahr*

Specification of *mahr* is not a necessary condition in permanent marriages. Therefore, if a man marries a woman without even hinting at a *mahr*, the marriage contract is valid. In fact, even if a man proclaims that he will not give a *mahr*, the marriage contract is still valid. Such a marriage is named *tafwid bud'*, indicating that determination of the marriage portion is postponed (Khomeini, 2004).

In temporary marriages, specification of a *mahr* is a necessary condition. If no *mahr* is determined, the marriage contract is invalid (ibid).

Article 1087: In a permanent marriage, if *mahr* has not been specified or lack of *mahr* has been set down as a condition, the marriage is still valid (Mansour, 2005).

Article 1095: In a temporary marriage, failing to specify a marriage portion invalidates the marriage (ibid).

This religious decree clearly indicates that what is important is effectuation of the marriage contract and even if no *mahr* is determined, or if both parties insist that there be no *mahr*, the contract is valid. Reevaluation of these decrees from a hermeneutic perspective sheds light on the purpose of the Originator of these decrees. *Mahriyah* is a trivial concern in permanent marriages. The second religious decree stated above indicates that in contrast to permanent marriages, *mahr* is of great concern in temporary marriages to such extent that failing to specify it invalidates the marriage contract. This is suggestive of the insignificance of *mahr*, and perhaps economic relations in general, when starting a long-term relationship. However, in short-term relationships, which are mostly based upon sexual relations and where weaker emotional bonds are formed, money and financial concerns play major roles. In such marriages, it is natural that the marriage portion should play a significant function and the lack thereof should cancel the contract. Putting these two decrees side by side makes it evident that the Legislator has placed great importance upon this matter. It was not an accident that *mahr* is peripheral in permanent marriage contracts.

These religious decrees have been expressed adequately in two articles of family law. In *Family*, Mutahari (1994) asserts that marriage is the heart of all other social connections and that *mahr* is a gift to help form an emotional bond of love between spouses.

In contrast Parsa (2001) and Moulaverdi (2007) believe that the importance of *mahr* must be emphasized and deny any methods of facilitating marriage that weaken the significance of *mahr*. For all that, Moulaverdi (ibid) holds that religious authorities who view *mahr* as a price (*thaman*) are showing disrespect towards women. She also believes that *mahr* must be paid in full at the start of marriage and that a law must be passed requiring men to pay all or half of the *mahr* at the outset of their married life, such as in Egypt (ibid). Parsa (2001) claims that it is always the rights of women that are violated; therefore, *mahriyah* must be clearly specified in the marriage contract and courts of law must duly punish husbands who do not pay the *mahr*.

Despite the fact that these ideas may mitigate the problem to some extent, they would undermine the very notion of marriage. Men would plainly see that in this relationship, money, or perhaps hard cash at the start of marriage, is more important than anything else.

The question that is disregarded in the approaches of Parsa (2001) and Moulaverdi (2007), one that is common among men in the society, is why men should bear such compulsory high costs. If this expense is based on the fact that men receive sexual enjoyment from the relationship and therefore must pay the price, the answer is that women also receive sexual gratification. In fact, some hadith claim that their sexual gratification is up to ninety-nine times greater than men (Ameli, 1967, p. 268). Undoubtedly, the need for sexual gratification is mutual and women also enter into married life due to this reason though it may not be the entire reason why a person, whether man or woman, gets married.

In any case, men cannot be forced to pay a sum in the form of *mahriyah* for sating their sexual desires. In the Western world, men do not give their wives money for such things, and life is not based on the fact that men fulfill their sexual needs. Such a view does not exist in the real world. In fact, in America, giving money in return for sex in any form is against the law (ProCon.org, 2010).

3. Amount of *Mahr* without Initial Determination (*Tafwid Bud'*)

> If a marriage occurs without previous determination of the marriage portion, the wife has no rights regarding *mahr* before

consummation of the marriage (Khomeini, 2004, p. 92).

Article 1093: In cases where a marriage portion has not been specified in the marriage contract, if the husband divorces his wife before consummation of the marriage and determination of *mahr*, the wife is entitled to *mahr al-mut'ah* (Mansour, 2005).

Article 1094: For determining the *mahr al-mut'ah*, the financial situation of the husband is to be considered (ibid).

This religious decree has been defined well in the law. However, in article 1093, the term *mustahaq* (is entitled to) is used whereas this same term is applied in article 1092[10] with a different meaning. Thus, the law has used a single term to mean two contrasting ideas. This usage of the term has resulted in lack of clarity in some articles

---

[10] Article 1092: "If a husband divorces his wife before consummation of the marriage, she is entitled to half of the *mahr*" (Mansour, 2005).

of the law. Even so, the issue of *mahr* is so common in courts and is discussed to such extent by both judges and lawyers that everyone understands the intent of the legislators. There is no reference to this ambiguous usage of the term *mustahaq* (is entitled to) in the research literature.

Here also the religious decree indicates that marriage itself is important and if the marriage is dissolved in some way (e.g. death of a spouse) before consummation and no *mahr* has been specified, there will be no *mahr*. Even in the case of divorce, the husband is only required to give a gift relative to his own economic situation as opposed to the status and situation of the wife. Katuziyan (1998), Damad (1990), and Imami (2008) consider this law to be fair but Parsa (2001) and Moulaverdi (2007) think otherwise.

Supporters of this law assert that it is not fair that a man who dies (or whose wife dies) before taking benefit from his married life be required to pay a *mahr* that has not even been settled between the two. Even if a man divorces his wife before consummation, it is still unjust to require him to give a *mahr* that is meant for a complete married life. Therefore, it is the responsibility of the man to give a gift—relative to his own economic situation—to the woman because of the divorce that he has engendered. After examining situations not considered by legislators, Damad (1990) still supports this item of the law.

Opponents of this law, including Moulaverdi (2007) and Parsa (2001), consider any harm to a woman's *mahr* to be unjust. They assert that divorce hurts women both socially and emotionally and naturally the husband, as the perpetrator of divorce, is responsible for paying damages. Therefore, the husband must give the complete marriage portion to the woman.

It seems that the first view is closer to equity. If women are to be considered faultless and oppressed in a failed relationship, there is no reason why men should not also be washed of any blame. Certainly, men are also faced with moral and social problems as a result of this failure.

If damages must be paid, it is fair that each of the parties pay damages to the other. In such a case, assessment of damages would be a complex matter. Regardless, Islam and the relevant law require men to make payment to women (a payment, not *mahr*) so as to end the matter.

A religious decree states that if a marriage is consummated without initial determination of *mahr*, the wife has a right to *mahr al-mithl*. This type of *mahr* is determined through reference to common customs and conventions as well as consideration of all aspects of the woman's status and situation. The customs the society or neighborhood the woman lives in is a factor in determining this *mahr*.

However, in modern times, with the existence of television and internet—and the complex social networks created by them—the world has become like a single village. Whatever happens in any corner of the world, everyone finds out. Thus, the customs of the neighborhood a woman lives in can no longer be considered since all the happenings as well as the political and social situation of this global village influence the behavior and decisions of families such that even the conduct of a Hollywood or Bollywood actor may affect the thoughts and behavior of the younger generation for a long time. Consequently, considering that large populations of Muslims live in Arab and African countries, the customary *mahr* would be much less than the *mahr* recommended by the Prophet (s), i.e. one-thousand dollars (Barakat, 1992). Thus, the customary amount of *mahr* must be determined as one-thousand dollars and common practice must not be limited to what happens within the borders of a country named Iran.

4. Payments Other than *Mahriyah*

Extracting payments and consuming such payments which have become traditional in some areas…is haram. The husband may reclaim it and, if it has been consumed, he may ask for compensation (Khomeini, 2004, p. 94).

This religious decree has not been considered in family law. It is necessary that legislators re-examine it. Again, religious law demonstrates that that the marriage portion does not possess an important role in married life. Only the opinion of the woman is important in this regard, not others. If the Divine Lawmaker had a different idea, He would perhaps respect native traditions and invite people to observe them. He would require husbands to pay costs other than *mahr* such as a bride price. This is not the case, however. Monetary or other requests of anyone other than the woman, such as her father or mother, for allowing the marriage are invalid. If a man is forced to pay, spending the money is haram for the person receiving the payment. This decree shows that God intends to facilitate marriage by absolving men of paying various costs.

Moulaverdi (2007) considers the demand for *shirbaha* (lit. price of milk) a consequence of the requirement for obtaining an adequate *jahaz* (household appliances and furnishings) for their daughters. She suggests that legislators consider the issues of *jahaz* and *shirbaha* as a part of the puzzle of social realities and set aside a part of *mahr* for the family of the woman. Some scholars advocate this view on the basis that it would facilitate marriage; however, Salehi (2002) and Imami (2008) believe that *shirbaha* has no legal or jurisprudential justification, and even if it does, it concerns the relationship between a mother and daughter and has nothing to do with a husband. Thus, they believe any connection drawn between *mahr* and other payments is inapposite.

It seems that Moulaverdi (2007) has overlooked the fact that in recent times, it is the men that show indifference towards marriage, one of the reasons of which is high marriage portions. If an amount is added to the marriage portion, which is supposed to be around one-thousand dollars but is often higher, for the woman to purchase household goods for the home of the newlyweds (*jahaz*), the low marriage rate will plummet even further.

Another solution must be found for *jahaz*. The costs of the marriage must not be obtained from *mahriyah* which is only a gift for the wife. Essentially, a broad perspective must be adopted encompassing all aspects of marriage including *jahaz*, *mahr*, *nafaqah*, and inheritance to be able to draw a suitable conclusion.

5. Specification of the *Mahr* by a Woman by Power of Attorney

> ...In this case, a woman can determine the *mahr* up to the *mahr al-sunnah*, i.e. five-hundred dirhams (Khomeini, 2004, p. 95).

> Article 1090: If a woman is given power of attorney to specify the *mahr*, she cannot stipulate an amount higher than *mahr al-mithl* (Mansour, 2005).

This religious decree stresses, once again, that the marriage portion must be limited to five-hundred dirhams. Specification of higher amounts is invalid. However, in the text of the law, the term *mahr al-sunnah* (the Prophet's tradition regarding *mahr*) has been exchanged for *mahr al-mithl* (fair dower). It is not clear why legislators deviated from the religious decree. Some scholars believe that the law must be amended (Damad, 1990). On the other hand, Azimzadeh (2008) declares that not only is the five-hundred dirham limit wrong, but even limiting *mahr* to the amount of *mahr al-mithl*, which is determined by common custom and conventions, is unjust. She believes that just as a man with power of attorney can specify any amount for *mahr*, a woman given power of attorney to determine the *mahr*, should be able to freely choose the amount (ibid).

On the surface, this view seems logical and just, but it is not in line with the aims of the religion. By referring to some of the numerous Hadith regarding this matter, all of which advise against high *mahr*, the purpose of the religion may be understood.

Of course, if a woman specifies a high amount as *mahr* and the husband agrees, there will be no problem. The religion raises no objection and no one can protest against this. The problem arises when the husband does not accept that figure. In this case, there are two options. Either the holy institution of marriage is shattered since the man does not accept the specified amount or the recommendation of Islam regarding *mahr* is put into force and the marriage continues.

6. Payment of Half the *Mahr* to the Husband

> If a woman frees her husband of the *mahr* he owes her and the husband divorces her before consummation of the marriage, the husband may demand half of the *mahr* from his wife... (Khomeini, 2004).

This religious decree does not have a corresponding legal article in Iranian family law. Therefore, persons affected by this decree are left confused. This interesting decree requires women to pay half of the *mahr* to her husband on several conditions.

Superficially, this decree does not seem very just. A woman absolves her husband of her *mahr* with good intentions. However, the couple reaches a stage where lack of the husband's love leads them to divorce. Now, she must give him something?

Imami (2008) believes that this decree, like other decrees regarding family, aims at strengthening the bonds of family and prevents divorce.

Asadi (2004) maintains that women who face this situation will consummate the marriage in order to avoid this happenstance, which may act as a cause for continuation of the relationship, development of love, and solidification of the marriage.

Both scholars see this Islamic decree as a preventive factor for divorce, similar to punishments that prevent people from perpetrating crime. On this assumption, the Divine Legislator's intent is that if a woman marries, reaches the point of divorce without even consummating the marriage, and absolves her husband of the *mahr*, she must be punished for her mistake of not being able to continue the relationship. Another advocate of this decree, Husaini (2009), prefers that this sum not be extracted from the wife and advises men to discharge them of this requirement.

One scenario regarding this decree is that a woman gets married but then decides that she does not wish to live with her husband. She asks her husband to divorce her and even agrees to free her husband of his debt so he does not worry about economic damages. In this case, the woman attains her purpose—divorce. However, Islam has a contrasting purpose. With this decree, Islam strives to invalidate such methods and strengthen the family institution.

Again, Parsa (2001) holds that this decree and others must be re-evaluated and it must never spread into the country's law. She argues that this edict is a relic of patriarchal thought that Islam strives to mitigate over time; however, in the patriarchal societies of the modern world, decrees that are completely in the interests of women are interpreted antithetically. In her view, this edict is comparable to the decrees regarding slavery in

Islam. Even though Islam is completely opposed to slavery, there are some decrees regarding this since time was required to abolish this practice.

In any case, it seems that since the correct amount of *mahr* is very low, it is not of paramount importance whether the husband must give it to the wife or vice versa in a long-term relationship necessitated by permanent marriage. Therefore, this decree also strengthens the hypothesis of low *mahr*. If the amount of *mahr* were high, this decree could result in the complete ruination of the woman and her family, which would be absolute injustice. This, however, is not the case and if a woman does give half the *mahr* to her husband, there will be no significant change in her life.

Results

This hermeneutical review of religious decrees has demonstrated the purpose of the Divine Lawmaker regarding the marriage portion and its amount. Therefore, *mahr* should not be allowed to be used for other than its divine purpose and become an instrument of women to prevent polygamy, divorce, or temporary marriages.

In previous sections, it was demonstrated many times that the Legislator has limited the *mahr* to about one-thousand dollars. This was a recommendation in some places and a requirement in others, a truth that has been neglected in Iranian family law and has led to heavy marriage portions.

Heavy marriage portions discourage men from seeking marriage and lead to a decrease in marriage statistics. This, in turn, prompts an increase in corruption. Moreover, even when marriage does occur, men feel threatened by the danger always overshadowing them that their heavy debts might be called in at any moment resulting in destruction of their lives (Kazemipur, 2010). They do not have a sense of security and this feeling increases with the knowledge of thousands of husbands who are incarcerated due to their inability to pay the *mahr* (Ebrat News, 2013).

If the family law limits *mahr* so as to realize the purpose of the Divine Legislator, we can positively hope for an increase in marriage and decrease in divorce rates. Also, it is recommended that the law require men to pay the *mahr* at the inception of the marriage contract so the wife can feel an amount of economic independence and the beginning of a feeling of complete security.

Chapter Two

The Daily Expenses (*Nafaqah*)

Introduction

Nafaqah is an Arabic term meaning donating and forgiving (Zubaidi, 1987). However, in Islamic terminology it refers to the expenses one has to cover for daily life. These expenses are normally covered by the husband (Al-Amili, 1983).

The matter of living expenses (*nafaqah*) is a controversial issue among Muslim spouses, especially Iranian ones. This argument has a darker color among the newer generations who have grown up with the alphabet of modernity (Mahdavi, 2007). Men question why a husband has to cover all the expenses in a joint life, which is supposed to be an unbiased union (ibid)?

A similar question is raised concerning the dowry and also other financial issues of marital life. It seems men cannot accept a model of marital life where one party is responsible for all the expenses and consider it unfair and unjust especially in the third millennium. Therefore, new methods for stopping this responsibility are being proposed, such as specifying a condition in the marriage contract so the husband has no commitment regarding *nafaqah* (Kariminiya, 1998).

Women, as it seems, only have problems with the mechanism of its practice rather than the idea and theory as a whole. It is rarely seen that women try to put a stop to *nafaqah* (Parsa, 2002). In fact, women have problems with receiving proper financial support (*nafaqah*), or any support at all, from their husbands (ibid), a point that will also be discussed in this research.

A simple sign of the depth and seriousness of this problem is the fact that the highest rate of divorce in Iran is related to this financial problem (Abhari, 2011).

According to Islamic rules about nafaqah, a husband has to take care of all of his wife's general expenses for living independently, costs of residence, meals, clothing and other necessities such as health care and transportation (Ameli, 2001). Husbands of the era of modernity ask what they get in return.

Sexual relations may be considered a reason husbands have to take care of all financial issues and daily expenses. Such relations and other possible reasons relate to both parties. The wife also takes benefit from such things. About sex in particular, according to Narrations women enjoy it several times more than husbands (Ameli, 2001). In a world where many people in modern and semi-modern countries have the mentality that a husband and wife both have to be responsible for daily living expenses, it is difficult to convince youths that current Islamic financial rules are just and closest to ideal life. These rules have not been updated to conform to the times. Even so, the prevailing state of affairs plays a very important role in *ijtihad* according to many scholars (Mutahari, 2013).

The problem of daily expenses (*nafaqah*) is somewhat more complicated than that of the dowry because the complications caused by the dowry could be solved by referring to the dowry amount specified by the Prophet, i.e. 500 Dirhams. Couples will not have serious problems leading to divorce if they continue the Prophet's recommendation in this regard (Zarchi, 2012). How can one explain the necessity for financial support of someone else for their whole life in the modern era only on the basis that they are partners or that they have sex with each other?

This is where, yet again, we need to take the hermeneutical view to discover the purpose of God, who has legislated these Islamic rules. God as the Legislator seeks to provide the best way of life for humanity in this world and a good existence in the Hereafter as can be seen in many verses and Traditions (Shabestari, 2010).

It is clear that rules must change based on circumstances of time and place. This is one reason why *mujtahids* have to be aware of prevailing conditions. When a *mujtahid* is thus aware, they can realize how general laws apply to the situation. Some religious authorities (*marja'*) consider this awareness an essential requirement without which a *mujtahid* is unable to become a *marja* (i.e. one who Muslims can refer to in religious issues) (Bahjat, 2012).

This is while other *maraji* (plural of marja) do not accept any change in decrees based on conditions of time and place (Shabestari, 1996). These scholars refer to a hadith by the Prophet emphasizing that what has been decreed as halal by Muhammad shall remain halal until the Day of Resurrection and what he has decreed as haram shall remain haram until the Day of Resurrection (Majlisi, 1989). Since felicity and happiness for humanity cannot be achieved without justice (Mohammadi, 1998), the issue of family expenses can be considered a pivotal point in Islamic rules and consequently the Family Law of Iran.

Assessing the Rules

The Islamic decrees[11] regarding *nafaqah* (living expenses) are presented in detail below. The relevant code in Iran Family Law is also provided for each rule. Finally, assessment and analysis is performed:

1. Conditions for Paying *Nafaqah*

Paying nafaqah or living expenses is obligatory (wajib) for any of the following three reasons: marriage, familial relationship, or ownership (Khomeini, 2002).

Code 1102: As soon as marriage properly takes place, the marital relationship will come into existence among the two parties. Thus, the rights

---

[11] The Islamic decrees will be taken from *Tahrir al-Wasilah* by Ayatollah Khomeini (2004) whose book is generally used as the main reference for Islamic decrees, especially in the lack of relevant laws according to article 167 of Iran's constitutional law.

and duties of the spouses towards each other will become valid and binding (Mansour, 2005).

In the above Islamic decree, three items make nafaqah obligatory. However, in the related legal code only marriage is stated as a requirement. The legal system does not consider the two other items here or elsewhere in the code of law (Asadi, 2001). Obviously, ownership refers to slavery which has been abolished. Even though familial relationship does not relate to our general purpose in this research, it is examined succinctly herein because it does indeed need to be indicated somewhere in the text of Family Law.

It is strange that law makers did not state the necessity of nafaqah with respect to familial relationships either in Family Law or elsewhere in Civil Law whereas some countries, such as England and France, have detailed chapters in family laws only for the expenses of children. These countries never had a brilliant source such as Islam to refer to (Mosaddegh, 2009).

There are some very useful Islamic decrees which are fully practical in the daily lives of Muslim families about nafaqah of relatives. These rulings discuss all angles of financial difficulties of families and how they may be solved. The Islamic framework is far more developed than the laws of aforementioned countries, but unfortunately it has been ignored.

One of them deals with cases where parents have to pay the living expenses of their adult children. For instance, where the children are able to work but cannot find work due to various reasons, such as not finding a job relevant to their dignity. Another example is the obligation of children (both sons and daughters) in paying nafaqah to their parents who are unable to take care of themselves financially. This obligation even continues down to grandchildren in the case that the children are absent (Khomeini, 2002, pp. 122, 126). This very important rule has not been considered in the Family Law. Neither Asadi (2004) nor Mosaddegh (2009) have pointed out this aspect of nafaqah when they were presenting and comparing positive British and French laws related to children. Moreover, none of the main family-related books of Katuziyan (1998), Asadi (2004) and Imami (2008) have examined this issue. Making allowances for these Islamic decrees could solve many problems in connection with poverty and even reduce crime if people knew about such a rule or were required to practice it as a law.

The term 'marital relationship' (*zujiyat*) that has been used in this code is ambiguous and therefore has different interpretations. At times—actually in many cases—lawmakers try to avoid direct use of terms relating to sexual intercourse to be more formal. This causes some difficulties for judges and lawyers in the interpretation and understanding of the exact intention of lawmakers. In this case, it seems the term 'marital relationship' refers to sexual relations, but some scholars controvert this.

Jafari (1976) believes it means sexual relationship while Safaii (1991) is convinced the term has a wider meaning, covering all relationships among the wife and the husband. Damad (2005) posits that it consists of all relationships and is not specific to sexual interactions only. He believes this can be understood from the terms 'rights and duties'. Due to the sensitivity of legal terms, it would be much more accurate if lawmakers attempted to simplify and clarify their terminology as much as possible so as to reduce such divergent interpretations among experts and scholars.

2. *Nafaqah* for Permanent Marriages

Paying daily expenses of a wife is obligatory on a husband only when the marriage is permanent. A wife in temporary marriage is excluded from obligatory payment of expenses. Another condition for the obligation is this that the wife be obedient to her husband. Of course, obedience to a husband refers only to cases that are obligatory. In such cases, a disobedient wife has no right to nafaqah. This rule applies whether a wife is Muslim or not (Khomeini, 2002).

Code 1105: In a spousal relationship, administration of the family belongs to the husband (Mansour, 2012).

Code 1106: A husband is responsible for nafaqah of a wife in permanent marriage (ibid).

Code 1108: A wife has no right to nafaqah if she denies her marital duties without a religiously valid cause (ibid).

Code 1113: A wife has no right to nafaqah in a temporary marriage unless nafaqah has been set as a marriage condition or the marriage has been taken place based on it (ibid).

The above religious decree has been spread out and described in four codes. This rule can actually define the foundation of discussions regarding nafaqah in marital relationships: obedience of a wife compensates for daily expenses (*nafaqah*) paid by a husband.

The balance of these key roles of spouses has been indicated in this Islamic rule, which has elucidated the duties of both parties toward each other. However, unfortunately such transparency cannot be seen in code 1108 which perfunctorily passes over the issue. The strange part is where definition of the term '*nafaqah*' has not been provided. Nevertheless, code 1106 makes use of the term where a duty is prescribed for the husband on the basis of that undefined term.

Two simple issues are understandable with a cursory look at the aforesaid Islamic rule and attached legal codes. First, in permanent marriage a husband is obligated to pay daily expenses (*nafaqah*) while it is not so in temporary marriages. Second, in temporary marriages obedience of a wife makes no sense because she is not paid for daily expenses and hadith has no direct indication of such a necessity (Ameli, 1984). The conclusion is simple: where nafaqah is paid, obeying the husband is obligatory (i.e. in permanent marriage) and where nafaqah is not paid there is no obligation for obedience to the husband (i.e. in temporary marriage).

The details of obedience is discussed in the Islamic rule below where it is concluded that the depth of this discussion only shows the special importance of the matter of obedience in nafaqah. One would expect the Iran Family Law to exercise more attention and care in such a critical subject and at least be more expressive regarding the issue of obedience and disobedience (Dayani, 2005).

Lack of proper consideration of this topic in the law has resulted in its gradual loss of importance in the society. This has prompted the belief among Muslim women that obedience to one's husband is a routine matter—more ethical than fundamental. It is not seen as a response to nafaqah (Allaee, 2004). Some scholars, however, disagree with the idea of nafaqah as a counterbalance to obedience (Dayani, 2005).

In the current situation, the society believes that nafaqah is inevitable and that there is no way to escape it because of the transparency of the legal codes. In explanation, there is no lack of law and this prevents people from shirking their duties. Those who attempt to avoid their responsibility toward nafaqah are naturally punished for their crime. On the other hand, women can escape their duties because there is no law or at least clear and transparent law in this regard and thus in the case of disobedience there is no discernable crime either. Since there is no relevant code of law, this type of misconduct (i.e. disobedience) becomes prevalent without giving people any guilty feeling because it has not been defined as a crime even though, religiously, it is. According to Dayani (2005), if a husband can be imprisoned why not a wife. He believes they must be imprisoned as well, according to clause 638[12] of the Islamic Penal Code, because their

---

[12] Article 638: Who ever does any haram action openly in public

actions are considered wrong and haram (Dayani, 2005).

This is a bilateral practice where nafaqah is offset by obedience. God as legislator of this mandate has assigned it purposely and with awareness so these elements can act as each wing in balanced, stable flight. If God has placed so much importance on nafaqah, it cannot logically be without a pairing side. This is why nafaqah is a daily practice as opposed to weekly, monthly or annually. In case a wife becomes disobedient, it is possible to discontinue nafaqah (Khomeini, 2002, p. 118).

Here is where the role of justice can be seen clearly. An answer to why all expenses of a wife have to be taken care of by the husband is that these two, i.e. payment of expenses by a husband and obedience of the wife, are intertwined. The

---

places, will be punished by a court penalty of ten days to two months imprisonment or seventy-four lashes... (Mansour, 2005)

mere presence of the wife as a spouse in the house is not enough.

Parsa (2002) has a differing view, however. Though she concedes that nafaqah belongs to an obedient wife, she maintains that the concept of obedience is limited only to sexual matters and does not cover other behaviors of a wife. Of course, this is not acceptable because the relevant Islamic rule has discussed this comprehensively with many examples.

3. Obedience and *Nafaqah*

If a wife disobeys and later becomes obedient again, this is not enough for her to deserve nafaqah. She has to announce her obedience openly until the husband becomes certain about it and an amount of time passes where she is available to her husband. Only then nafaqah becomes obligatory for the husband again (Khomeini, 2004, p. 114).

Disobedience by a wife occurs when the wife digresses from the criteria of obligatory obedience to her husband. For example, she does not allow her husband access or avoids matters relating to the husband's lust and enjoyment...[13] (Khomeini, 2004, p. 102)

---

[13] A wife's refusal to use make-up or adorn herself when her husband expects it is considered disobedience. Leaving the house without the husband's consent and similar issues are also instances of disobedience. Disobedience does not cover items that are not duties of a wife according to the religion so if she avoids things and tasks, such as housework, that have nothing to do with the pleasure and joy of the husband, it is not considered disobedience. Refusal to do tailoring, cooking and similar tasks, even giving water to the husband if he asks or doing the bed is not considered disobedience of the type that negates nafaqah (Khomeini, 2002, p. 102).

[13]If some signs of disobedience occurs from the wife, if her behavior and habits change in speech and action, for instance she used to always speak kindly to her husband and answered his questions nicely but now speaks harshly or she always smiled but is now moody and does not answer the husband's questions without asking a few times and eventually answers with rage and so on, the husband has to advise her and if she does not listen to his good advice then she is considered disobedient... (ibid)

Code 1108: A wife is not qualified for nafaqah if she desists from fulfilling her marital duties (Mansour, 2012).

As is apparent from the selections above, the religious ruling has a profound difference with the clause in Family Law concerning discontinuance of nafaqah.

Obedience and nafaqah are both sensitive issues and must be examined in like manner.

Disobedience to a husband may be divided into two types. One relates to the sensual side of a marital relationship while the other concerns general obedience, covering permission to leave the house, behaving nicely with the husband, and fulfilling his requirements and desires. The second type is what scholars imply when discussing the broader aspect of obedience (Damad, 2005).

As might be expected, such complete obedience to a husband raises a serious question. This kind of obedience only can be found among slaves or bond servants, and the slavery era has long past. Obedience where the wife has to absolutely obey the husband is far from moral (Anon., 2013).

The basis of this claim is correct and it needs to be considered as there is no reason for a human to obey another human to this extent and be fully under another's control. Therefore, such expectations of a wife seem inhuman and unethical, and need to be amended.

On further reflection, however, this puzzle has other pieces which help making sense out of the concept of obedience. By examining the society, it is clear that this type of obedience is in practice almost everywhere causing no problems in social relationships other than marital ones. It mainly holds true where a person is hired for taking care of certain issues. As an extreme example, those who work in the military have much similarity to a wife in the area of obedience. Soldiers knowingly enter the contract to follow orders fully and never disobey in anything (unless illegal), otherwise severe punishment will ensue. Soldiers agree to abstain from disrespect towards their superior officers and have to observe military formalities. Soldiers have no right to ask the simplest question concerning orders and have to fully obey else face punishment (USAPD, 2005). Soldiers accept to perform difficult tasks and live in severe conditions even for months at a time in remote desserts or forests. It seems that if their salaries were cut off, all but a few would not only deny the abovementioned grueling activities but would also stop taking the simplest of orders.

Another example is companies and organizations. Basically, many people are paid for obeying orders even if they dislike the activities or hate them, as in the saying money talks.

In any event, the ethical aspect of this issue is beyond the scope of this research. Some examples were presented to show the leading role of money in daily life. It is apparent that marital life is different than army life or being an employee.

According to Islamic rules and Family Law, a wife must be paid and logically there has to be a reason for the wife deserving such payment. Even the idea that the reason of such payment is the sex a husband receives makes the problem much worse and unethical. Also, if somebody supports other members of their family financially (e.g. sisters or brothers) and in return only gets disobedience and unkindness, they would probably stop their support.

Be that as it may, many female researchers, such as Mohamamdi (2004) and Allaee (2004), insist that there are serious problems in reception of nafaqah and thus more force needs to be placed upon husbands. They fail to notice, however, why husbands are not motivated to pay. They do not realize that an eagle cannot fly with one wing no matter how much one pushes it.

Given that Family Law has discussed marital duties very generally without clearly specifying its nature, problems have arisen in practice causing much oppression in the society among both men and women. It has caused oppression because it has upset the balance of the financial relationship in marriage specified purposefully by the religion to harmonize the marriage. The Family Law left the concept of "marital duties" vague where it was time to talk about what a husband receives in return for paying nafaqah to his wife. This led to abandonment of the rights of husbands by not only common people but also lawyers, judges and even the judicial system (Anon., 2013).

The Family Law needs to amend these codes to help youths find a simple answer to their aforementioned question about the reason for covering all daily expenses. Not having the answer to this question may have significant negative effects such as the increase of divorce and avoidance of marriage. Regardless, the answer is now clear and simple: the husband has something to expect in return for his expenses.

4. Amount of *Nafaqah*

There is a particular amount defined by the religion for nafaqah. A Muslim husband is obligated to prepare whatever the wife needs, such as food, clothes, beds, carpets, a place of residence, servants, necessary tools and equipment for cooking, drinking, cleaning, etc. (Khomeini, 2002)

...but the amount of the meal has to be an amount that makes her full and has to be based on what people like her normally eat in her town. It must be compatible with her normal diet and has to be what she is used to eating and would get sick otherwise...[14] (ibid, p. 116).

---

[14] "...even if her meal is always meat. It is obligatory to prepare such meals for her and also other things that if she does not eat, drink or use would cause her damage or sickness, such as tea, coffee, tobacco, etc. and especially fruits of all seasons particularly

Code 1107: Nafaqah includes housing, clothes, meals, and house equipment which are suited to the wife's status, and a servant if she is used to having a servant, if she is sick, or if she lacks a part of her body (Mansour, 2005).

This Islamic rule makes what was explained in the previous item clearer about why nafaqah with all its details is necessary and why Muslim husbands have to provide such services to their wives. By comparing the duties side by side, one can easily understand the justification and logic behind these two heavy responsibilities (i.e. that a husband covers his wife's financial expenses at least to the mentioned extent and that the wife is

---

the summer fruits which are necessary in the heat. Regarding clothes, her habits have to be respected in quantity and texture, exactly according to what other women from her town are used to, both for summer and winter clothes, because the difference between the clothes of women in each city, family, quantity, quality and texture are great. If the Muslim's wife is from wealthy family, it is obligatory for him to prepare her fancy outfits as befit her station rather than just normal clothes..." (Khomeini, 2002, p. 116)

obedient to her husband at least to the obligatory extent). Upon further consideration, one can see the subtleties to this rule. For instance, if a wife is in the habit of drinking a particular coffee at a certain time, the husband has to prepare it for her or if she dresses in luxury outfits, they also have to be obtained for her at the same level of luxury. The obligations of a husband can be understood from code 1107 even though it has presented a brief explanation.

In return though, there is no description of the obligations of a wife concerning obedience. This imbalance, according to Mahdavi (2007) and Dayani (2005), destabilizes the relationship between spouses, ruins nafaqah from the foundation, and drives husbands toward direct or indirect avoidance of paying nafaqah. When a husband sees he has to cover all the expenses of a person who is disobedient, he tries to divorce her or if not possible, he may prefer to continue the situation he is caught in by not paying all her daily costs. Still, Allaee (2004) and Pourabdollah (2013) contend that disobedience has nothing to do with the reason husbands escape their duties. They believe some sort of mechanism has to come into play that makes no escape possible for men. Among their solutions, having the nafaqah paid directly by the court is the boldest.

A hermeneutical assessment of this issue shows that Islam intends to provide financial security[15] to women and a feeling of comfort[16] to men. If law makers seek justice and religion, they need either to remove nafaqah from the law or add in necessity for obedience along with sufficient description.

It needs to be mentioned that code 1105 discusses administration of the husband in the marital

---

[15] Q: 4:34 "Men are the protectors and maintainers of women, because Allah has given the one more (strength) than the other..." (Yusuf Ali, n.d.)

[16] Q: 30:21 "And among His Signs is this, that He created for you mates from among yourselves, that ye may dwell in tranquility with them, and He has put love and mercy between your (hearts): verily in that are Signs for those who reflect" (Yusuf Ali, n.d.).

relationship but due to the lack of transparency and the shortfall in portrayal of the boundaries thereof, it has lost its applicability and basically does not mean anything, especially when there is no penalty for a failing wife.

Adding conditions to the marriage formula has been explained in code 1119; however, it does not directly relate to the subject of nafaqah. Even so, it can be used by the husband by stipulating the condition that nafaqah will be stopped immediately in case of the wife's incorrect behavior. Thus, a husband can make a personal law for his own marriage and put into practice the rules that Islam has already specified. At the same time, Kariminiya (1998) believes the opposite claiming that nafaqah is a definite law that one cannot change or cancel by specifying a condition in this regard whereas most Ayatullahs such as Khuii (2013), Khomeini (2004) and Sistani (2013) and many scholars such as

Katuziyan (1998), Asadi (2004), Imami (2008) believe otherwise.

Unfortunately, once again lawmakers have ignored the required balance among the parties in this code and once again they have taken the women's side by bringing some examples which can be imposed as conditions. There are four examples, all to the benefit of the wife and not even a single example concerns the husband's benefit. It is apparent that this code also needs to be amended to at least look a little more unbiased. This unjust act of the lawmaker has been neglected by both supporters and opponents of nafaqah whose works have been assessed in this research.

5. Daily *Nafaqah*

The wife owns the nafaqah of the same day which the husband is responsible for. This does not include the nafaqah remaining left over from the day before. If anything does remain, it belongs to the husband. A wife's ownership of the nafaqah of each day is not solid and remains variable. It is based on the condition of obedience...[17] (Khomeini, 2002).

Regrettably this Islamic rule has not been considered in Family Law either, not even briefly. The society follows in the footsteps of the lawmakers and ignores the Islamic rules which seem unimportant to them. This means that disobedience (*nushuz*), which is the opposing side of nafaqah, is insignificant or possesses low significance for families and the society does not consider it worth discussion. This is exceedingly

---

[17] "...The wife can request her nafaqah every day and if the husband does not provide it to her before the day ends even though she is obedient, the nafaqah will be a debt of the husband to his wife. The husband owes her as long as she is obedient whether she requests her nafaqah or not, whether a judge has specified the amount of the nafaqah for her or not, and whether the husband is rich or poor. In the case of poverty, the husband will be given some time to become wealthy enough to pay his debt. As for the nafaqah of forthcoming days, no wife may request it because it does not yet belong to her" (Khomeini, 2002).

apparent in the lives of couples today and causes people to make fun if one raises the issue that nafaqah does not apply to a disobedient wife.

Chapter Three

Wages for Housework and Work outside the Home

Introduction

Another important issue in the financial relationship between husband and wife is the work of the wife either inside or outside the home. This issue includes efforts of wives to obtain the right to receive wages for housework along with full permission to work outside of the home in whatever type of work they desire whenever they want. According to code 336 of Iran's family law, such a request can be claimed only if the husband submits a divorce request, but this is not what women want.

In codes 1117 and 336, Iran's family law has stated the conditions for the work of the wife. The former discusses the husband's rights to stop his wife from working outside the home and the latter puts forth the right of the wife to receive wages for housework.

With regard to this, one problem that exists is that men are asking why the husband must both cover household expenses and also pay the wife when she works in her own home. Also, men want to know why, according to the law and according to Islamic rules, the husband has to pay all the expenses from the money he makes while the wife can keep all the money she makes without any duty to share in any expenses (Mahdavi, 2007).

The root of these two issues, which are completely related to one another, can be found under the same topic in the previous chapter, entitled *Nafaqah*—which deals with the husband's duty to pay all expenses and all financial commitments in return for having his marital needs met by his wife.

As covered in the section on disobedience (*nushuz*), any activities on the part of the wife which cause difficulties for the husband in having access to her for his marital needs is forbidden (*haram*). The final result presented in the conclusion of the previous chapter had the same core issue, full obedience verses full financial support. The husband wants to have access to his wife whenever he desires and wants her to be cheerful and act kindly; in return, he must meet her needs as well, and financial support is the main foundation for this trade off. The same issue and core reason exists here. The husband covers all the costs of living so that he can have his wife beside him and not have to wait some hours for her to return home tired so he can fulfill his marital needs.

Consequently, the husband can forbid his wife from working outside or even from leaving the house in order that his needs are met. However, at the same time, when the wife complies and does housework at home, while she is able to work outside and make money for herself, somebody has to be responsible for this loss on the part of the wife. Of course, it is the husband who must compensate for the wages that she loses as the result of his request of her to remain home. The wife fulfils her marital duties at home and the husband must provide full financial support in return; however, if the husband adds an additional requirement to his wife—housework—he also has to be responsible somehow for this new request and must compensate for it. This very accurately shows the justice inherent in Islamic rules.

Nevertheless, the desire of women to work outside the home still remains. According to Islamic rules (Khomeini, 2003) and Iranian law (Anon., 2013), women have full rights for ownership over their own properties. History shows that Islam has recognized this right for over fourteen hundreds years while in Europe and even France only in recent decades have such rights been accorded to women (Saeidi, 2010). It can be seen that, in the absence of compensation, there might be a serious conflict between the rights of men and women—the husband's right to have his wife in the home and the wife's right to ownership, doing business and developing and expanding her properties which obviously depend mainly on being able to go out of the home.

Husbands often disagree with their wives working outside, first of all, because they see they have no right to their wife's revenue and, second of all, because they have to wait much of the time to see their wives and in the end they see a tired wife who has no energy for her husband, the children or housework. This being the case, why shouldn't husbands disagree?

In this chapter the Islamic rules related to these two issues will be assessed along with the related legal codes of Iran's family law.

Lastly, if we consider justice the basic and final goal of Islamic rules (Shabestari, 2010) taking a hermeneutical view, the balance of the scale of justice has to be equal; accordingly, not paying the wife for the work she performs in the house imbalances this scale.

Assessing the Rule

> One of the husbands' rights from his wife is that the wife obey him and not leave the house without his permission even though she intends to visit her relative or visit her sick father or attend her father's funeral... (Khomeini, 2002, p. 100)

> Code 1117: The husband can prevent his wife from performing a job which conflicts with his or her interests or the interests of the family. (Mansour, 2012)

As is clear from these quotes, the husband's consent is so important that the wife cannot even attend her father's funeral without permission. The legal code has explained the interests of the husband, wife and family as key towards allowance of the wife's work. There is a vast difference between the legal code and the religious decree because, according to the decree, the husband does not need to have any particular reason and as he desires he can stop his wife from leaving the house either for work or in general. However, according to the legal code, the husband has to provide his reasons to the court to prove that he is right and his wife's work conflicts with his interests putting his reasons at the risk of not being accepted by the judge.

Of course, a wife can specify conditions for the right to work, place of residence etc., in the original marriage agreement, but this issue is outside of our discussion and we intend to review the situations of most wives herein rather than exceptions.

Damad (2005) has cited the sensual passions as grounds for the husband to ban his wife from working. Damad (ibid) narrates from *Minhaj al-Salihin* of Sayyid Hakim that any activities that can cause problems in this regard can be blocked by the husband such that the wife can be prohibited from working outside the home and even from undertaking a home based business at her computer.

The opinions of scholars (*maraji*) are conflicting according to judiciary system reports. While some strongly support the opinion of Ayatollah Khomeini as stated above, others give a completely opposite judgment (Anon., 2005).

Taheri (2009) and Hedayat (2007) state separately in their articles that there should not be any wage *(ujrat al-mithl)* paid to wives in Iran because of the absence of this convention among the people and in view of the fact that this legal code is ruining the normal lives of families.

On the other hand, Ahmadiyeh's (2009) opinion disagrees with Taheri (2009) and she believes that women must be paid a normal salary according to the union rate and that this is the minimum she deserves in view of the fact that she is able to earn money but is being banned from doing so.

The foundations of Ahmadiyeh's (2009) opinion are correct based on religious decrees and family law because anyone who works must be paid and whoever prevents one from earning is responsible for lost revenues. However, the second part of her opinion, where she asserts that the wage has to be at union rates is debatable. It is easily understandable that the job a woman does at home is different from working in a factory, school or even an office. For the latter, she must commute back and forth from home to work every day; there are costs for transportation (tickets or gas etc.); there is the risk of accidents; there are extremes of hot and cold weather that must be tolerated; and, most importantly, there are greater job responsibilities, while nowadays at home the wife can watch an interesting TV program while doing the cooking or talk to her friends while she is vacuuming, etc.

Housework is much easier today than it was a thousand years ago, or even 30 years ago, due to the prevalence of technological devices and household appliances, and what used to take a few hours each day can now be done in a few minutes every week. As a result, the average time spent on housework is a lot less than what is spent on work outside which also entails the other difficulties mentioned above. Of course, an increase in the number of members in the household—children, grandparents, etc.—can increase time spent on housework, but households are changing nowadays and there are not many families with five children or more as in previous decades (Anon., 2013).

Jalali (2011) has chosen a middle course and believes that if the husband gives permission to his wife to work outside, he will no longer be responsible to pay wages for housework. It seems that he is trying to set a balance by giving one right in return for another right. His idea seems to be practicable if the husband were to accept that such a deal is fair because the wage a woman can make working outside is a lot more than the money she can earn for housework. This means the housework can be done by a worker for two of three hours every day or so but the wage for such is not comparable with the wage a woman gets when she works 8 hours outside, so husbands may feel they are losing in the deal especially when they have to face a tired wife at the end of the day.

Taheri (2009) considers any type of payment to the wife completely unfair while the husband is required to work, earn money and pay all the expenses of the wife and household, such as rent, food, clothing, etc. and must additionally pay something on top of that to the wife as wages for her work in the household.

Results

According to the assessment in previous chapters, the husband must accept the responsibility of full financial support if he wants to have the full obedience of his wife. If the husband wants his wife to stay at home and not work outside, this is his right because he supports her financially i.e., pays for all expenses of the house, meals, clothes, etc. However, if he also wants her to work in the home—when she can work outside for herself and keep the money for her own use—then he has to accept that he must also pay for this work on a monthly basis, as long as he does not decide to divorce her. If lawmakers change legal codes 1117 and 336 such that they are compatible with the Islamic decree, we can expect the balance to return to the marriage. In order to facilitate this process, the government can encourage husbands by waiving their taxes up to a certain point, if they pay wages to their wives through the banking system into some long term governmental investment projects. This can help all three—the wife first, the husband and the government.

Conclusion

By comparison of relevant religious decrees and family law codes, differences have been discovered. The goal of this research was to provide some solutions for reducing the rate of divorce and increasing the rate of marriage through hermeneutical review and assessment of religious decrees and related family law codes.

Accurate discovery of these dissimilarities was a step in assessing opinions of other researchers and finally providing relevant solutions for amending deficiencies in Iranian family law. The differences discovered in this research show that the current financial problems related to divorce are linked with the areas where differences exist.

This comparison shows that the main reasons for divorce are financial; particularly, the high amount of *mahr* and failure to pay *nafaqah*. There are areas where differences and dissimilarities are greatest between religious decrees and codes of family law.

Even though the Iranian family law gains its roots from religious decrees, it interprets justice differently from the religion. There are equivalent responsibilities for each spouse, and even though the textures are different, the weight of each is the same.

Such a combination of Islamic decrees and non-Islamic views can have no result except chaos in courts and within families. In order to avoid this problem, it is necessary that the law chooses a clear path. Either a secular perspective has to be implemented in the law where both women and men have fully equal rights and responsibilities, or a fully Islamic view must be put into play. In the secular option, all the costs of living and other financials issues along with rights concerning guardianship of children need to be completely equal. In this case, family law would deviate from religious goals and utilize secular justice. It is not truly possible to effectuate this method since the majority of the population of Iran is Muslim.

The other option is for the law to embrace religious decrees and harmonize itself with religious aims. Incomplete implementation of religious decrees in the family law causes much harm to families and the society as a whole. It also gives the people the wrong impression that the religion can no longer be put into practice in today's world.

Also, it is necessary for the government to choose a specific policy towards family law. The administration must either let it be free based on the people's own decisions within the general religious framework or set some solid procedures for every single code. Either the government has to stop getting involved in the details of the private relationships of people and their marriages, or it has to get involved in details. Either approach can be helpful. In the first case, after a while the society will come to the conclusion that if they set heavy marriage portions or husbands do not pay *nafaqah*, there is no law to support them and put their husbands in prison. Therefore, the society will slowly lean towards a more logical *mahr* and wives will lean toward obedience to their husbands if they want to receive their *nafaqah*.

If the government decides to get involved in the details, then it has to set more specific laws for current problems such as high *mahr* and failure to pay *nafaqah*. The government has to limit the *mahr* to around 1,250 dollars and also set some procedures for proper punishment of husbands who do not pay *nafaqah*. Not only this, but it must also set punishments for the wives that are not obedient.

The government can encourage husbands to pay their wives wages for working in the house. Encouragements can be in the form of additional facilities, tax waives, loans, etc. if the husband pays the wages though the banking system in an account in their wife's name.

In conclusion, the government needs to do serious reassessment of family law, and amend it to bring it closer to religious decrees.

Bibliography

Abhari, M., 2011. *Heavy Dowries, the Cause of 85% of Divorces.* [Online]
Available at: http://www.jahannews.com/vdcamwn6a49now1.k5k4.html
[Accessed 7 May 2013].

Ahmadiyeh, M., 2009. Nihlah and Ujrah al-Mithl. *The Book of the Women,* pp. 292-320.

Al-Amili, Z. a.-D., 1983. *Al-Rudha al-Bahiyah fi Sharh al-Lum'ah al-Damishqiyah.* Qum: Bahman.

Allaee, F., 2004. Barrasi Tahliliyeh Ghavamiyat. *Mahnameh Daneshgah al-zahra,* pp. 24-56.

Ameli, H., 1967. *Wasa'il al-Shi'a: Abwab Mohor.* Beirut: Ehya Torath al-Arabi.

Ameli, H., 1984. *Wasa'il al-Shi'a.* Beirut: Al al-Beyt.

Ameli, H., 2001. *Wasa'il al-Shi'a.* Qum: Jameh Modaresin.

Anon., 2005. Report of the Research Center. *Dadrasi,* p. 51.

Anon., 2013. *Divorce Rate.* [Online]
Available at: http://vista.ir/article/228361
[Accessed 2013].

Anon., 2013. *Ownership.* [Online]
Available at: http://www.alqaza.com/far/index.php?option=com_content&view=article&id=879&Itemid=
[Accessed Aug 2013].

Anon., 2013. *Religious Questions.* [Online]
Available at: http://www.askdin.com/thread14155.html

Anon., 2013. *The Crime Status.* [Online]
Available at: http://www.dchq.ir/html/index.php?name=News&file=article&sid=2682
[Accessed 2013].

Anon., 2013. *The Gloom of Legal Terms.* [Online]
Available at: http://www.iranbar.org/pm33.php
[Accessed 20 7 2013].

Asadi, L., 2001. Barrasi Nafaqah Zoojih dar Englis. *Nedaye Sadiq,* pp. 8-30.

Asadi, L., 2004. The Analysis of Women's Legal Approval. *The Quarterly Magazine of the Cultural and Social Council of Women,* Volume 10.

Avvo, 2012. *Divorce Statistics.* [Online]
Available at: http://www.avvo.com/legal-guides/ugc/marriage-divorce-statistics

Azimzadeh, F., 2008. Brief Review of the Dowry. *Nedaye Sadiq,* Volume 21, pp. 40-52.

Azizi, M., 2003. Mehri Dar Mehriyeh Nist. *Aroose Honar,* Volume 27.

Bahjat, M. T., 2012. [Online]
Available at: http://www.bahjat.org/index.php/ahkam-2/esteftahat/94-2011-09-06-09-16-55.html

Bahonar, M., 2011. *The Dowry Over 110 Gold Coin Won't Have Prison Sentence.* [Online]
Available at: http://www.ma-delavar.parliran.ir/index.aspx?siteid=1&pageid=2964&newsview=13667
[Accessed 7 May 2013].

Barakat, H., 1992. *Family and Society.* [Online]
Available at: http://acc.teachmideast.org/texts.php?module_id=8&reading_id=13&sequence=7
[Accessed Aug 2013].

Damad, M., 1990. *Dr.* Tehran: Nashre Ney.

Damad, M., 2005. *Juricprodential Review of Family Law.* Tehran: Nashr Ulum Islami.

Dayani, A., 2005. Rabeteh Tamkin va Noshooz. *Mizan,* pp. 7-15.

Ebrat News, 2013. *Ebrat News.* [Online]
Available at: http://ebrat.ir/?part=news&inc=news&id=51655
[Accessed August 2013].

Feyz, M., 1983. *Mafatih al-Shara'ih.* Qum: Jameh Modarresin.

Ghafariyan, S., 2011. The Problems of Dowry. *The Women*, pp. 121-140.

Habibi, M., 2003. The Importance of the Dowry in Marriage. *Marifat,* Volume 118, pp. 85-96.

Hedayat, F., 2007. The works of the women and family. *Woman and Economy,* pp. 25-46.

Husaini, S. M. B., 2009. Mehriyeh Ebra Shodeh. *Dadrasi,* Volume 75.

Imami Namini, M., 2006. The nature of the heavy dowries. *Noormags,* pp. 31-44.

Imami, M., 2008. Nafaqah Zan Bardar. *Fiqh,* pp. 90-162.

Iranian Drug Control Headquarters, 2013. *Crime Statistics.* [Online]
Available at: http://www.dchq.ir/html/index.php?name=News&file=article&sid=2682
[Accessed 2013].

Jafari, L., 1976. *Family Law.* Tehran: Moalif.

Jalali, S. M., 2011. *Critical Women Study,* Volume 48.

Kariminiya, M., 1998. Soghoote Nafaqah. *Dadrasi,* pp. 60-64.

Katouziyan, N., 1998. *Civil Family Law*. Tehran: Ney.

Kazemipur, S., 2010. *The Average Amount of the Dowry of Iranian Women*. [Online]
Available at: http://www.mashreghnews.ir/fa/news/5629/450-%D8%B3%DA%A9%D9%87-%D9%85%D8%AA%D9%88%D8%B3%D8%B7-%D9%85%D9%87%D8%B1%D9%8A%D9%87-%D8%B2%D9%86%D8%A7%D9%86-%D8%A7%D9%8A%D8%B1%D8%A7%D9%86%D9%8A
[Accessed 6 May 2013].

Khomeini, R., 2002. *Tahrir al-Wasilah*. 4th ed. Qum: Dar al-Ilm.

Khomeini, R., 2002. *Tahrir al-Wasilah*. 4th ed. Qum: Dar al-Ilm.

Khomeini, R., 2003. *The Purchase Book*. Tehran: Nashre Asare Imam.

Khomeini, R., 2004. *Tahrir al-Wasilah*. Tehran: Nashre Asare Imam Khomeini.

Khuii, A., 2013. [Online]
Available at: http://lib.eshia.ir/10143/2/67/%D8%A7%D9%84%D9%85%D9%87%D8%B1
[Accessed 2013].

Langaroudi, J., 2004. *Family Law*. Tehran: Kaatib.

M. Shabestari, 2010. *Hermeneutics, the Book, the Tradition.* Tehran: Tarhe Noo.

Mahdavi, I., 2007. Ravabete Zujain. *Hoghoogh dar Islam,* p. 43.

Majlisi, A.-L., 1989. *Usul al-Kafi.* Beirut: Ihya Turath.

Makarem, N., 1996. Tafsire Nemooneh.

Malekzadeh, F., 2009. Assessment of the Dowry in the Iranian Family Law. *Women Social Study,* pp. 33-53.

Mansour, J., 2005. *The Collection of the Civil Laws and the Rules.* Tehran: doran.

Mansour, J., 2012. *The Collection of Civil Law.* Tehran: Douran.

Mohammadi, 1998. *Ghadha va Ghidhavat dar Islam.* Tehran: Sayeh.

Mohammadi, M., 2004. Ezdevaj, Nafagheh, Tamkin. *Ketab Zanan,* pp. 180-213.

Mosaddegh, S., 2009. Nafaqag Zoojeh Dar Fiqh Imamiyah. *Rahnemoon,* pp. 115-137.

Moulaverdi, S., 2007. The assessment of the The Dowry 's principle. *The Law of the Women,* Volume 14, p. 6.

Mutahari, M., 1980. *Majmoeh Asar.* s.l.:Bita.

Mutahari, M., 1994. *the Law System of Woman in Islam.* Qum: Shahid.

Mutahari, M., 2013. *Ijtihad Definition.* [Online]
Available at: http://islampedia.ir/fa/1390/04/%D8%AA%D8%B9%D8%B1%DB%8C%D9%81-%D8%A7%D8%AC%D8%AA%D9%87%D8%A7%D8%AF/
[Accessed 2013].

Parsa, F., 2001. Some Discussion in the Rights of a Wife. *Human siences Journal of al-Zahra University,* pp. 61-88.

Parsa, F., 2002. Mabahesi Dar Haghooghe Zoojeh. *Faslanem Pajooheshi Daneshgahe al-Zahra,* pp. 62-84.

Pourabdollah, K., 2013. Mabani Feghhi Nafagheh. *Fiqh Nedaye Sadegh,* pp. 150-173.

ProCon.org, 2010. *Prostitution.* [Online]
Available at: http://prostitution.procon.org/view.resource.php?resourceID=000119
[Accessed Aug 2013].

Qarai, n.d. *Tanzil.net.* [Online]
Available at: http://tanzil.net/
[Accessed August 2013].

Raqib, 1983. *Ghamous Mofradat.* Beyrout: s.n.

Saeidi, M., 2010. *Journal of the Faculty of Law and Political Science.*

Saeidipur, H., 2001. *The Collection of 12 Marajih.* Qum: Saba.

Safaii, H., 1991. *Family Law.* Tehran: Mizan.

Salehi, M., 2002. Some discussion for Family Law. *Dadrasi,* Volume 32, pp. 41-46.

Seyyed Murteza, 1996. *Al-Intisar.* Qum: Jama'ah Mudarresin Qum.

Shabestari, M., 1996. *Ghera'ate Rasmi Az Din.* Qum: s.n.

Shabestari, M., 2010. *Hermeneutics, the Book, the Tradition.* Tehran: Tarhe Noo.

silverpriceoz.com, 2013. *http://www.silverpriceoz.com/silver-price-per-kilo/.* [Online]
Available at: http://www.silverpriceoz.com/silver-price-per-kilo/
[Accessed August 2013].

Sistani, 2013. [Online]
Available at:
http://www.sistani.org/index.php?p=251364&id=48&pid=2349
[Accessed 2013].

Tabatabaii, 2000. Tafsir al-Mizan. In: s.l.:Jameh Modaresin Qom.

Taheri, B., 2009. How much is the woman's wage in the house?. pp. 75-93.

USAPD, 2005. *Manual for Courts-Martial Article 92: Failure to obey order or regulation,* s.l.: s.n.

Yousofzadeh, H., 2005. Receiving the Social Effect of the Dowry. *The Book of the Women,* pp. 48-60.

Yusuf Ali, n.d. *Tanzil.net.* [Online]
Available at: http://tanzil.net/
[Accessed August 2013].

Zarchi, A., 2012. *Removing the Dowry from Iran Family Law.* Tehran, Foreign Ministry Digital Publication.

Zubaidi, M., 1987. *Ghamoos Taj al-Aroos.* Beirut: s.n.

www.ingramcontent.com/pod-product-compliance
Lightning Source LLC
Chambersburg PA
CBHW072217170526
45158CB00002BA/642